CONSTELLATIONS

E.M.HANS

RAINTREE
STECK-VAUGHN
RSVP PUBLISHERS

A Harcourt Company

Austin   New York
www.steck-vaughn.com

CONSTELLATIONS

Other titles in the series: Comets and Asteroids ●
● The Earth ● The Moon ● The Solar System ●
● Space Mysteries ● Space Travel ● The Sun

Published by Raintree Steck-Vaughn Publishers,
an imprint of Steck-Vaughn Company

Library of Congress Cataloging-in-Publication Data
Hans, E. M.
Constellations / E. M. Hans.
    p.   cm.—(Spinning through space)
    Includes bibliographical references and index.
    ISBN 0-7398-2743-X
    1. Constellations—Juvenile literature.
    [1. Constellations.]
    I. Title: Constellations. II. Title. III. Series.

Printed in Italy. Bound in the United States.
1 2 3 4 5 6 7 8 9 0 05 04 03 02 01

CONTENTS

THE NIGHT SKY

When you look up at the night sky on a clear, cloudless night, you will see the stars. They are suns, like our own sun, but they are at least a million times farther away. Away from the lights of a city, you will see the whole sky full of brilliant points of light. You might see a faint hazy pattern of light, called the Milky Way, making an arch overhead. You will feel that you can almost reach out and touch the stars. Each one has a different name and place in space. If you want to find your way around the sky, you must learn the patterns the stars make.

▲ Constellations are groups of stars that make patterns in the sky. These pictures are from the Northern Hemisphere.

Think of groups of stars as dots in a puzzle that join to make a picture. These star pictures are called constellations. Many of the names of the constellations we use today come from the Ancient Greeks and Romans. Dividing the stars into constellations helps us locate different stars in the night sky.

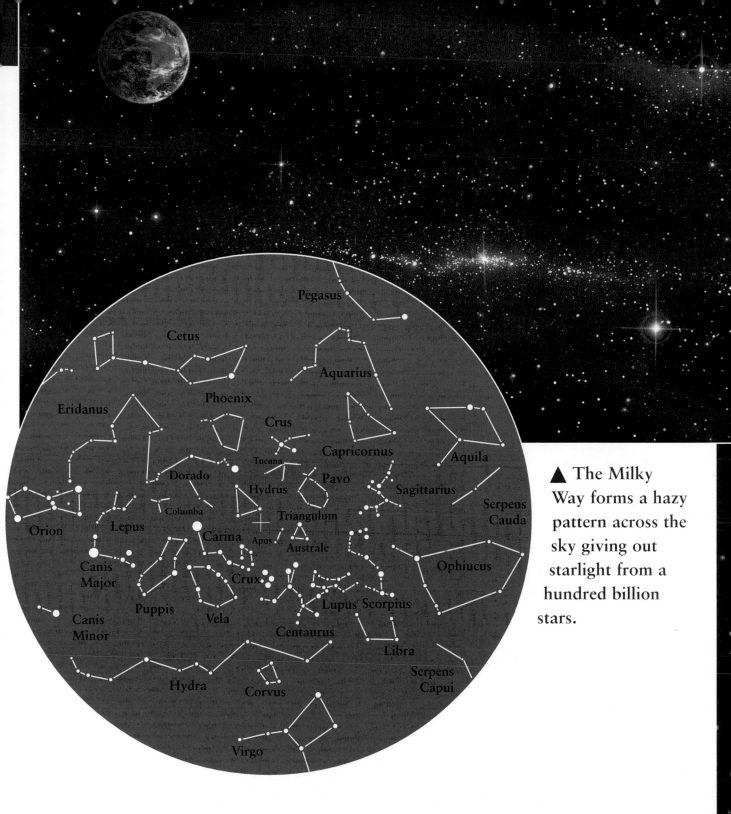

Pegasus

Cetus

Aquarius

Phoenix

Eridanus

Crus

Capricornus

Tucana

Aquila

Dorado

Pavo

Sagittarius

Hydrus

Serpens
Cauda

Columba

Triangulum

Orion

Lepus

Carina

Apus

Australe

Canis
Major

Crux

Ophiucus

Puppis

Vela

Lupus Scorpius

Canis
Minor

Centaurus

Libra

Hydra

Corvus

Serpens
Capui

Virgo

▲ The Milky
Way forms a hazy
pattern across the
sky giving out
starlight from a
hundred billion
stars.

▲ This is the pattern of
many of the constellations
from the Southern
Hemisphere.

Many other peoples in different countries
throughout history have also played the
connect-the-dot game in the sky and have named
their own star pictures.

For people who live in different parts of the world, there are certain stars that are seen all year-round. In the Northern Hemisphere they are called the northern circumpolar stars because they surround the North Pole. In the Southern Hemisphere, a different set of stars is seen around the South Pole, known as the southern circumpolar stars.

The Great Bear

One of the best known star pictures in the northern sky is Ursa Major, which means "the Great Bear." The seven stars of the Big Dipper are part of the Great Bear. They are formed from the tail and hips of the Great Bear. Close to the Great Bear is her son, the Little Bear (Ursa Minor). This constellation is close to the position of the North Pole and includes the North Star.

According to Greek mythology, the Great Bear and Little Bear were thrown into the sky by their tails by the king of the gods, Zeus, to save them from hunters. Because their tails were stretched, the bears have "long tails."

▲ Star pictures, such as the shape of the Great Bear, still guide us around the night sky.

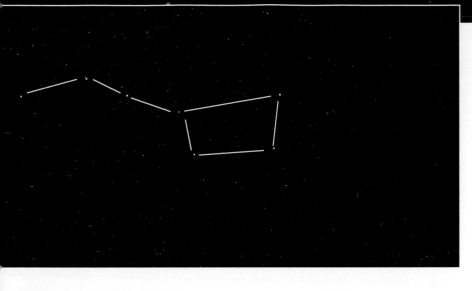

◀ In the United States, these seven stars were thought to make up the shape of a water dipper.

▼ Crux is the most famous constellation of the Southern Hemisphere—forming a clear cross in the sky. It is known as the Southern Cross.

The stars in a constellation are usually not near each other in space. They are just in the same part of the sky as we see them from Earth. If we looked at the stars of the Great Bear (or Little Bear) from another part of the galaxy, they would make a completely different pattern.

The Southern Skies

Many of the constellations seen in the Northern Hemisphere are also seen in the Southern Hemisphere in the same month of the year. But they are seen in a different part of the sky. The star patterns seen in the north are "upside-down" when viewed in the Southern Hemisphere. The circumpolar constellations of the Southern Hemisphere include Crux and Centaurus.

THE SKY THROUGH THE SEASONS

The constellations seen in the skies are more easily visible in some months than others. To look at stars, you need to view them on a dark, clear night. Use the star maps on pages 4–5 to help you find the positions of the constellations.

In the Northern Hemisphere, the circumpolar constellations include Ursa Major and Ursa Minor.

Northern Spring/Southern Fall

The constellations in the evening sky at this time of year include Leo the lion, Virgo the maiden, and Corvus the crow. Leo is easy to find. Look for a star shaped like a question mark the wrong way around. This is the head and mane of Leo. Imagine the lion lying down with his front paws stretched out before him and his tail curled over his back. Behind Leo is a forked shape. This is Virgo the maiden. In Greek mythology she is Persephone, the goddess of the spring. Close to Virgo is Corvus the crow.

▼ Some of the constellations visible in the northern spring and southern fall.

Leo   Virgo   Corvus

Northern Hemisphere		Southern Hemisphere	
Northern spring	Leo Virgo Corvus Hydra Cancer Boötes Corona Borealis	Southern fall	Leo Virgo Corvus Hydra Cancer Vela
Northern summer	Cygnus Lyra Aquila Delphinus Hercules Scorpius Sagittarius (Ophiucus)	Southern winter	Cygnus Lyra Aquila Delphinus Hercules Scorpius Sagittarius Hydra Boötes Corona Borealis Grus

Northern Summer/Southern Winter

▼ Some of the constellations visible in the northern summer and southern winter. The individual stars Vega, Deneb, and Altair are shown as star shapes in the illustrations below (left to right).

Northern skies are dominated by a bright triangle of stars called Vega, Deneb, and Altair. Each one is in a different star picture, so if you find the "summer triangle," you have located three more constellations. Vega is in a constellation called Lyra, which represents a lyre, a musical instrument like a small harp. The star Deneb is the tail of Cygnus the swan, and Altair is the bright star in Aquila the eagle.

Lyra   Cygnus   Aquila

Northern Hemisphere		Southern Hemisphere	
Northern fall	Pegasus Andromeda Cetus Perseus Boötes Corona Borealis (Pisces) (Aquarius)	Southern spring	Pegasus Andromeda Cetus Grus Piscis Austrinus Capricornus (Pisces) (Aquarius)
Northern winter	Orion Canis Major Canis Minor Taurus Auriga Gemini (Lepus) (part of Eridanus)	Southern summer	Orion Canis Major Canis Minor Taurus Auriga Gemini Perseus Puppis Lepus

▼ Some of the constellations visible in the northern fall and southern spring

Northern Fall/Southern Spring

Look for the constellation of Andromeda. In Greek mythology, Andromeda was a princess rescued by Perseus from the sea monster Cetus, who was turned to stone. Three of the stars of Pegasus and the end star of Andromeda make up the Square of Pegasus. This is easy to spot, because it is one of the biggest geometrical shapes in the night sky. Andromeda also contains the Great Spiral Galaxy.

Andromeda　　　　**Cetus**　　　　**Pegasus**

Northern Winter/Southern Summer

In the Northern Hemisphere, Orion the hunter can be seen clearly. Look for three stars almost in a row. This is Orion's belt. There are two stars marking his shoulders and two more stars for his knees. Follow Orion's belt southward away from this constellation and you will come to the brightest star in the night sky, Sirius the dog star. It is in Canis Major, the great dog. Making an equal-sided triangle with Sirius and Betelgeuse, (Orion's shoulder), is the star Procyon. Procyon is the brightest star in Canis Minor, the little dog. The star called Aldebaran is the eye of Taurus, the bull.

Orion's belt forms a distinctive part of this constellation.

▼ Some of the constellations visible in the northern winter and the southern summer. The individual stars Sirius, Procyon, and Aldebaran are shown as star shapes (left to right).

Betelgeuse

Rigel

Canis Major

Canis Minor

Taurus

DISTANCE TO THE STARS

The stars that make up constellations provide a pattern that helps us remember which star is which, but they do not tell us about the stars themselves. To learn what the stars are really like we have to look at them more closely. The most obvious thing about stars is that they have different brightnesses. However, they are also at different distances from us. If we want to know how bright a star really is, we need to know how far away it is.

▼ Early astronomy in the observatory at Greenwich, England. One observer takes measurements while another uses a telescope to view the sky.

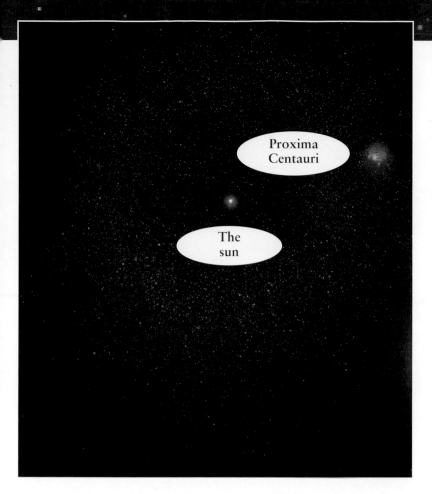

Proxima Centauri

The sun

▲ Proxima Centauri is the nearest star to the sun. It can only be viewed from the Southern Hemisphere with a telescope.

Understanding Parallax

To understand what parallax is, try this experiment. Cover your eye with your left hand. Now stretch your right hand out as far as you can, and with one finger block out an object on the other side of the room. Don't move the finger but change your left hand to the other eye. The finger will appear to have moved. This is because your point of view has changed. Do the same again but with your right hand nearer your face. The finger will appear to have moved even more. The amount the finger seems to move depends on how far away it is from your eyes. This is called parallax.

Hipparcos (190–120 B.C.) developed the method of trigonometry and used it to measure the lunar parallax, the distance from the Earth to the moon.

In the same way, as the Earth moves around the sun, our viewpoint changes. Nearby stars will appear to change position against the background of more distant objects. This shift, called parallax, allows astronomers to calculate how far away the stars really are.

How Far to the Stars?

The distances to stars are huge. They are so big that we need a new way to measure them. We can measure distances on the Earth in miles or kilometers. Distances between planets are in millions of miles or kilometers, but the distances between stars are at least a million times bigger than that.

A convenient way of thinking about enormous distances is in terms of the length of time light would take to travel from one point to another. Light is the fastest thing in the Universe. It travels at about 186,000 mi. (300,000 km) per second. That is about seven and a half times around the world in a second. It takes over eight minutes for light from the sun to reach the earth, which is 93 million mi. (150 million km) away.

▲ The satellite Hipparcos was the first satellite to produce an accurate map of the positions of more than 100,000 selected stars in space.

A light-year is a measure of distance, not time. One light-year is the distance light travels in one year, roughly a distance of 5.5 trillion mi. (9 trillion km).

The dog star, Sirius, in Canis Major, is the brightest star in the sky. It is 8.6 light-years away.

Light from the "nearby" star Sirius takes more than eight and a half years to travel through space to us. If you think about the difference between a minute and a year, it will give you an idea of how far away stars are.

When you look up at the night sky, the starlight you see has been traveling across space for thousands, even millions of years.

A nearby star's distance can be calculated using the principle of parallax—measuring its position twice, six months apart, when the Earth is positioned at opposite sides of the sun.

FEATURES OF STARS

The radius of Betelgeuse is hundreds of times bigger than the sun.

Once we know how far away a star is, it is easy to figure out how bright it really is. Some stars, like Sirius, look bright because they are relatively close to us.

Others, like Rigel in Orion or Betelgeuse look bright because they truly are massive headlights in the sky.

▲ Betelgeuse is a massive red supergiant. It is the tenth brightest star in the sky, at least 5,000 times brighter than our Sun.

Colors

Another difference between stars is their colors. If you look carefully at stars, you should be able to see different colors. Some stars like Betelgeuse and Aldebaran are red. Arcturus is orange. Vega and Rigel are blue. Sirius and Altair are white, and the sun is yellow.

Their color tells us how hot stars are at their surface. Red stars are the coolest at 5,400° F (3,000° C). Yellow stars like the sun are around 10,830° F (6,000° C), white stars 18,030° F (10,000° C). The hottest of all are the blue stars. Blue stars can be up to 36,030° F (20,000° C) and even hotter in extreme cases to over 54,030° F (30,000° C).

By knowing how bright a star is and how hot it is, astronomers can calculate how big it is. Very large stars, hundreds of times as big as the sun, are called giants or supergiants. Small stars are called dwarfs. The sun is a yellow dwarf.

The blue supergiant Rigel, in Orion, is 140,000 times brighter than the sun.

Our sun is a ball of hot gas 870,000 mi. (1.4 million km) across. It is a yellow dwarf.

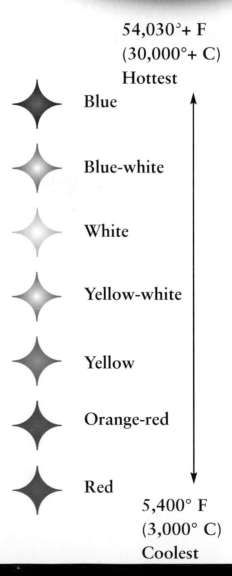

54,030°+ F
(30,000°+ C)
Hottest

Blue

Blue-white

White

Yellow-white

Yellow

Orange-red

Red

5,400° F
(3,000° C)
Coolest

▶ Red stars such as Aldebaran are the coolest, while blue stars such as Rigel are the hottest.

THE STORY OF A STAR

When we look at the sky carefully, we see much more than just stars. There are also huge glowing clouds of gas and dust called nebulae, like the great nebula in the sword of Orion or the North American nebula in the constellation Cygnus. These are really "star factories."

▼ Nebula in Orion. This is a starbirth region 1,500 light-years from Earth.

The birth of a star

Swirling nebulae of dust and gas are the birth of stars.

Gravity pulls the gas together, and a spinning disk is formed.

Nuclear reactions begin with enormous energy.

The star spins, and the dust and gas become flattened in a ring around the star.

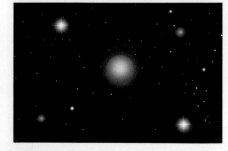

Finally, the new star is formed.

The Birth of Stars

The center of a cloud begins to pull in the edges by the force of gravity so that the whole cloud shrinks down to form a spinning disk. As it does so, it becomes hotter. A star begins to form, taking up most of the material. Around it, planets and moons are formed by the rest of the gas and dust.

The first stars were probably formed over 12 billion years ago when the universe came into being.

As the star grows, pulling in more and more gas, it eventually gets so hot and so squashed in the center that a nuclear reaction starts and the star begins to shine. When that happens it blows away almost all the rest of the gas and dust around it.

Stars give out a lot of energy as light and heat.

The Death of Stars

Our Sun has a life span of 10 billion years.

▼ This is a dying star in nebula Lyra. The white dwarf in the center has blown its outer layers into space.

Within a large star, there is a battle between gravity and the outward pressure of heat. As hydrogen runs low in the core, the star sheds layers of gas. Eventually the core collapses. This can take the form of a tremendous explosion called a supernova that tears through the star as it dies. The death of a star is one of the most spectacular events of the universe.

▲ This is how an artist imagines an exploding supernova would look.

Dying Sun

Smaller stars like the sun reach their ends less dramatically. The sun was formed over five billion years ago. In another five billion years, the sun will have burned up all the hydrogen gas that it uses as nuclear fuel in its core. It will expand to engulf the planets Mercury and Venus and probably the Earth, too. Finally it will puff off its outer layers and shrink down to become a very hot dense star called a white dwarf. This will slowly cool over millions and millions of years.

All the debris left after the death of the sun, including everything that is left of the Earth, will be recycled into the next generation of stars and planets.

GROUPS OF STARS

A nebula often produces more than one star. Stars that orbit around each other are called double or multiple stars and are very common. In fact it is single stars like the sun that are scarce. Most of the stars you can see in the night sky are double or multiple. Both Sirius and Procyon have white dwarf stars orbiting around them.

Some years ago it was suggested that the sun had a companion star called Nemesis, but it has never been found.

Double stars are held together by gravity. It is difficult to tell these stars apart without using a powerful telescope.

▼ The Alpha Centauri double star. These stars orbit each other every eighty years.

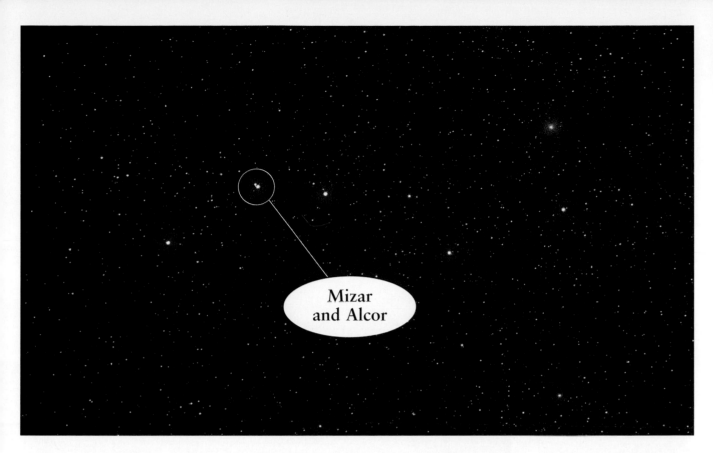

Mizar
and Alcor

▲ The star Mizar and its companion, Alcor

The star Mizar in the Big Dipper travels through space with a much fainter companion, Alcor, that is close by. If you look through a small telescope, you will see that Mizar itself is a double star.

Albireo, the eye of Cygnus (see Cygnus the swan on page 9), is a particularly beautiful double star. One star is sapphire blue, while the other is golden yellow. The star Castor in the constellation of Gemini is multiple. What we see as one star is actually at least six stars, all orbiting around each other in a complicated gravitational dance. Life on a planet in such a system would be very interesting with six suns in the sky!

Astronomers study the orbit of double (binary) stars because this information can be used to calculate the masses of the two stars.

Star Clusters

The Greeks said that there were only six bright stars in the Seven Sisters, because the seventh sister was in mourning for the city of Troy, which had been destroyed by a Greek army.

Very large nebulae can make whole clusters of stars. An easy cluster to spot is the Pleiades, or Seven Sisters, in the constellation of Taurus, the bull. If you look at the Seven Sisters on a clear moonless night you should be able to see six bright stars. With binoculars or a small telescope, you will see dozens of "sisters." The very largest telescopes can show about 500 stars.

▼ The Pleiades, or Seven Sisters cluster. The cluster contains young, blue stars.

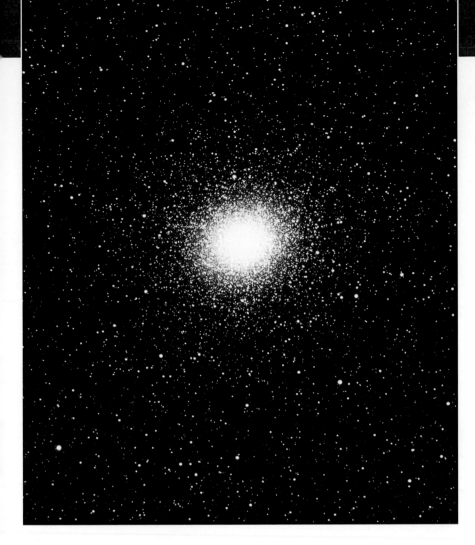

▲ Omega Centauri in the constellation Centaurus is the brightest globular cluster in the galaxy.

There is another cluster in Taurus that is also easy to see. The stars that make up the V-shape of the bull's head (see page 9) are part of a cluster called the Hyades. The star Aldebaran, the bull's eye, is not part of the Hyades. It is roughly halfway between Earth and the cluster. You can tell that the Hyades are closer to Earth than the Seven Sisters, because the Hyades cluster looks bigger in the sky than the Seven Sisters and the stars appear farther apart.

Globular Clusters

Globular clusters can contain a million stars.

The Hyades and Pleiades are called open clusters. They are made up of bright, young stars. But there is another type of star cluster. It is called a globular cluster. Globular clusters contain some of the oldest stars in the Milky Way. They are found around the outside of our galaxy.

GALAXIES

The Milky Way

All the stars, clusters, and nebulae discussed so far are part of our galaxy, the Milky Way. Seen edge on, the Milky Way is a flat disk shape with a bulge of stars in the middle called the nucleus. The globular clusters are scattered in a sphere around the disk. This is called the halo of the galaxy.

The solar system revolves around the middle of the Milky Way about once every 225 million years.

▼ The Earth is part of the solar system, which is part of the Milky Way, which is part of a bigger cluster of galaxies.

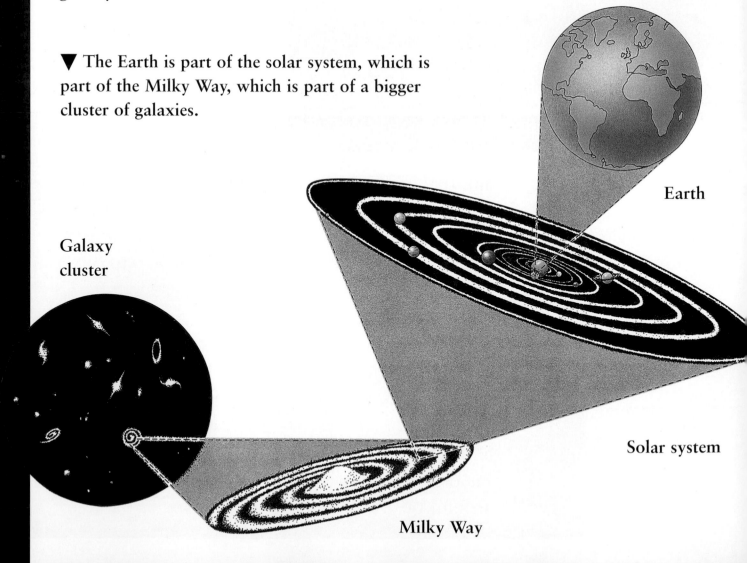

Galaxy cluster

Earth

Solar system

Milky Way

▲ Our Milky Way measures approximately 100,000 light-years across.

The disk is where the open clusters, nebulae, and most of the stars, particularly the youngest ones, are found. They are not spread out evenly on the disk. Rather they make a sort of spiral pattern like a pinwheel or a whirlpool. The solar system is not in the center of the galaxy. It is in one of the spiral arms two-thirds of the way from the center out toward the edge of the disk.

The center of the Milky Way lies in the direction of the constellation Sagittarius, the archer. We cannot see the center because there is so much gas and dust in the way. All the stars, gas, and dust orbit around the center of the Milky Way, just as the planets orbit the sun.

Sagittarius contains more stars than any other constellation because the center of the galaxy lies in that direction.

▶ A spiral galaxy has a bright center with arms of stars curving out in a spiral shape.

▼ Elliptical galaxies vary in shape from circular to oval.

More Galaxies

When we use a large telescope to look beyond the stars of the Milky Way, we can see many other galaxies. They come in different shapes and sizes. Many are ordinary spiral galaxies like the Milky Way. Some are barred spirals, where the spiral arms start from a bar of stars extending on either side of the nucleus. Others are elliptical. They may be small or huge with hundreds of times as many stars as the Milky Way. Some galaxies have no particular shape. These are described as irregular.

▶ Irregular galaxies are often smaller than elliptical or spiral galaxies and do not have a well-defined structure.

◀ Andromeda and the Milky Way are part of a cluster of galaxies called the Local Group.

Across the Universe

The closest large galaxy to the Milky Way is Andromeda. It can only just be seen without a telescope. It looks like a faint, hazy patch in the sky. Galaxies form larger groups, called clusters. The Milky Way and the Andromeda galaxy are part of a cluster called the Local Group, which stretches three million light-years across space and forms part of an even larger supercluster. This is just one of many other superclusters stretching for many millions of light years across the universe.

The Andromeda galaxy is approximately 2.9 million light-years away as measured by the Hipparcos satellite.

GLOSSARY

Astronomers People who study the science of the universe.

Binary stars Two stars that revolve around each other, locked together by gravity.

Circumpolar Stars that revolve around the poles.

Clusters Groups of stars or galaxies that lie close to each other.

Dwarf star A star that is relatively small.

Elliptical Shaped like a flattened circle.

Galaxy A massive group of stars, dust, and gas, drawn together by gravity.

Globular cluster A group of a few thousand to a million stars that form the "halo" of our galaxy.

Gravity A force that attracts a smaller object to a larger one.

Hemisphere Half of a sphere, such as the northern or southern part of the Earth.

Hydrogen An invisible gas with no color or smell.

Light-year The distance that a ray of light travels in a year; over 5.5 trillion mi. (9 trillion km).

Lunar To do with the moon.

Mass The amount of matter in an object, measured in pounds (kg).

Milky Way A broad band of light in the sky created by the millions of stars that make up our galaxy.

Nebula A cloud of gas or dust in space.

Nuclear reaction Atoms of gas in a star joining to make larger atoms, creating heat and light.

Nucleus The center of an object, such the dense part in the middle of a galaxy.

Radiation The waves of energy, heat, or particles from an object.

Trigonometry The branch of mathematics that deals with the relationships between the sides and angles of a triangle.

FURTHER INFORMATION

Web pages:

www.emufarm.org/~cmbell/myth/myth.html
The Mythology of the Constellations

starchild.gsfc.nasa.gov/ Star Child: A
Learning Center for Young Astronomers.
This site is geared toward young people
with an interest in astronomy.

Books to read:

Mitton. Jacqueline. *Zoo in the Sky: A
Book of Animal Constellations.*
National Geographic Society, 1998.

Scott, Elaine. *Close Encounters:
Exploring the Universe with the
Hubble Space Telescope.* Disney
Press, 1998.

Taylor, Helen. *You'd Never Believe It
But...There's a Great Bear in the Sky
and Other Facts About Stars.* Copper
Beech Books, 1998.

Thompson, C. E. *Glow-in-the-Dark
Constellations: A Field Guide for
Young Stargazers.* Grosset & Dunlap,
1999.

Places to visit:

National Air and Space Museum
7th and Independence Ave., S.W.
Washington, D.C. 20560
(202) 357-2700
www.nasm.edu

NASA/Kennedy Space Center
Kennedy Space Center, FL 32899
(407) 452-2121
www.ksc.nasa.gov

INDEX

All numbers in **bold** refer to pictures as well as text.

Picture acknowledgments:
The publishers would like to thank the following for allowing their pictures to be reproduced in this book: Bruce Coleman/Astrofoto 6; Eye Ubiquitous cover (inset top); Mary Evans Picture Library title page; Genesis 14; HWPL 7 (both), 12; Science Photo Library 18, 22/Celestial Image Picture Company cover (inset middle), 29, /Julian Baum 13, /Chris Butler 27, /John Chumack 16, /Luke Dodd 25, /David Ducros 5, /David A. Hardy 28,/Mehau Kulyk 21, /Pekka Parviainen 23, /Ronald Rover cover (main), 24, /John Sanford 15, /Robin Scagell 11, /Space Telescope Science Institute/NASA 20 and cover (inset bottom). Artwork by Peter Bull Art Studio except page 26 (HWPL).